The Testimony of Integrity

in the Religious Society of Friend

Wilmer A. Cooper

Pendle Hill Pamphlet 296

About the Author

Wilmer Cooper grew up among Conservative (Wilburite) Friends in eastern Ohio. He is a graduate of Olney Friends School and Wilmington College. His education includes graduate degrees from Haverford College, Yale Divinity School and Vanderbilt University. During World War II, he did alternative Civilian Public Service under the American Friends Service Committee. In the 1950s he was Associate Secretary of Friends Committee on National Legislation in Washington, D.C. He joined the faculty of Earlham College in 1959 and was the founding Dean of the Earlham School of Religion. Following eighteen years as Dean he became Professor of Quaker Studies until his retirement in 1985. He has continued teaching part time and writing on Quaker subjects. He is the author of two books, *The ESR Story: A Quaker Dream Come True, 1985,* and a new book, *A Living Faith: A Historical Study of Quaker Beliefs,* published by Friends United Press, 1990. He and Emily Cooper live in Richmond, Indiana and part of the year in Florida. They are members of West Richmond Friends Meeting, Indiana Yearly Meeting, and are the parents of four children and five grandchildren.

This essay on "The Quaker Testimony of Integrity" is an expansion of addresses given on the subject before several Friends groups, including two yearly meetings. It has been published in abbreviated form by *Friends Bulletin* of Pacific, North Pacific and Intermountain Yearly Meetings, a flyer by Northwest Yearly Meeting (Evangelical), and a June,1988 article in *Friends Journal* in Philadelphia.

ISBN 0 87574 - 296 - 3

Library of Congress Catalog Card Number 91-060175

March 1991: 5,500
March 2002: 1,000

Several years ago I invited the well-known British Friend, Elfrida Vipont Foulds, to address my Quakerism class at Earlham School of Religion. Elfrida Foulds began by telling how she had several years earlier wrestled with "The Message of George Fox" when she had been asked to give a talk on the subject. Although she had spoken on it many times before, she said that as sometimes happens to a writer or speaker, "her subject went cold on her." So in an attempt to bring it alive she considered several alternatives. She could go up to London and do further research at Friends House Library, or in the British Museum. She could climb Pendle Hill where Fox had a vision of "a great people to be gathered." Or she could traverse the Westmoreland countryside where George Fox had come to meet Margaret Fell at Swarthmoor Hall. But none of these alternatives seemed very promising.

Then it occurred to Elfrida Foulds to go back to the birthplace of George Fox at Fenny Drayton in the English Midlands to seek the inspiration she needed. So the next time she went up to London on the train she got off at Nuneaton and made a side trip to Fenny Drayton, a sparsely populated village. As she walked around the village she realized that probably only one building was still standing that was there when Fox was a boy, and that was the village church. So she went over to the church, pushed open the large door and went in. She took a seat on one of the front pews and decided to sit there in meditation. She lapsed into absolute silence, no sound within or without. Finally she saw in her mind's eye the boy George Fox sitting there with his family in the church, Sunday after Sunday, worshiping. But the boy George looked puzzled; he seemed to be pondering why he and his family, and their neighbors, came week after week to the village church where they prayed; where they made solemn affirmations; and where they witnessed to Christ. But then the self-same people would go from the church the following week cheating their neighbors, cheating in the marketplace; they would get drunk in the ale houses; husbands would beat their wives and parents would cuff their children. Next Sunday they would faithfully go back to the village church and go through the same religious exercises as the week before, only to repeat the same kind of behavior in the village the week following.

All of this inconsistency troubled the boy George Fox so that he continued to ask deep questions about the meaning of life, given this kind of behavior. At this point Elfrida Foulds says that the message of George Fox suddenly came to her, namely, that Fox felt the need for integrity in daily life. He saw that there must be a correspondence between one's faith, between what one professed on the Sabbath, and what one does during the daily work week.

The upshot of all this, says Elfrida, was that Fox believed he must speak the truth at all times. He had to say "yes when he meant "yes," and say "no" when he meant "no, without quibbling. If he said he would do a thing, he would do it. If he said he would not do it, he would not. As Fox searched for answers to life, he searched the Scriptures; he talked to the priests of the surrounding countryside; he frequented the steeple houses (as he called the churches of his day); but the one thing he kept coming back to was the need for integrity in daily life.

So "integrity" became the subject for the message of George Fox which Elfrida Foulds was to deliver. She pointed out that Fox continually tested what integrity meant in his own life. For example, when friends invited him to a drinking bout, he refused because he saw an inconsistency between such behavior and the faith he proclaimed. Fox also saw many inconsistencies when he observed the churches of his day. He believed that a minister of the gospel could not be prepared at Oxford or Cambridge, if such persons were not also moved by the promptings of the Holy Spirit, the voice of God within. Moreover, Fox refused to call places of worship "churches" because a church is not a building; it is the people of God; it is the fellowship of believers. The church is the men and women who come together in worship; therefore, Friends called their places of worship "meetinghouses" rather than "churches."

Another story reflects my convincement about Integrity as the basic Quaker testimony. In the winter of 1980 I was on sabbatical leave at Woodbrooke, the Quaker study center in Birmingham, England. A young woman in residence from India was studying at Birmingham University nearby. Because she had never met any Quakers before coming to Woodbrooke, she understandably wanted to find out more about them. Someone suggested that she ask me, a visiting Friend from America giving some lectures. When we met she began by asking me, "What is a Quaker?" and "What is Quakerism?" Because I didn't have a quick and simple answer, she became impatient with my hesitant response. Unfortunately, I began with the usual professorial response by suggesting that she read a couple of Quaker writings in the Woodbrooke Library, and then we would get together and talk about it. At this point she began to show strong displeasure, if not anger. All she wanted was a straightforward, two-sentence answer to "What is a Quaker?" and, "What is Quakerism?"

As I have struggled with this question then and on many occasions since, as probably most Quakers have, it occurred to me that perhaps the word "integrity" comes as close as any single-word answer to, "What is Quakerism?" I claim that "integrity" is the essential Quaker testimony and undergirds all other testimonies of Friends in relationship to Quaker faith and practice. If integrity is to serve as a shorthand way of describing the essence of Quakerism, it must find its root in the context of Quaker history. I want to unearth that root in the remainder of this essay.

The Meaning of the Quaker Testimonies

Without a doubt one of the unique characteristics of the Religious Society of Friends is what we have called the Quaker testimonies. We might refer to them as the Quaker equivalent of the creeds of the churches, though the intent of testimonies is primarily ethical rather than doctrinal. The claim is that the testimonies grow out of our inward religious experience and are intended to give outward expression to the leading of the Spirit of God within; or put another way, they are formed by the voice of conscience illumined by the Light of Christ within.

From the beginning Friends believed that they could have direct and immediate communication with God which would enable them to discern right ethical choices. But they soon experienced certain common leadings of the Spirit which became formalized into testimonies. These testimonies served as common principles and standards of behavior and action which they believed the consistency of the Spirit's leading required of them. At the same time they believed that they must be convinced of the "truth" of the testimony each time they were called upon to enact it in their lives. Otherwise the testimonies would become lifeless rules of conduct, which then would be "out of the truth."

In his 1990 Swarthmore Lecture *Testimony and Tradition,* John Punshon describes his understanding of the testimonies :

> Inwardly they are our guide to the nature of our Creator, the source of our inspiration, the medium of our understanding. . . . Externally they are our guide to life, a sign of the divine love for creation, the means

> of our prophetic witness. They therefore take their meaning from the highest reality we know. [Punshon further says,] . . . we have to look for the root of the testimonies in the inner life, not the outer (Punshon, *Testimony and Tradition*, 94, 49).

There is no definitive list of Quaker Testimonies. They have differed throughout the history of Friends. Some of the early testimonies included the refusal to pay tithes to the Church of England; the refusal to take oaths before judges; the refusal to bow to superiors and pay hat honor. Friends also practised the testimony of plainness in personal dress and the furnishing of their houses. In addition they practised the testimony of "plain language," thus addressing persons in the singular, "thee" and "thou," instead of the plural form, which signified social distinction. Further, the "plain language" required that they designate the days of the week and the months of the year numerically, rather than by the pagan names of pagan gods. By the same token Friends did not observe special holidays and seasons of the Church year, not to mention the secular holidays of the State. They believed that every day was "the day that the Lord hath made" and therefore was to be kept holy. This meant no celebration of Christmas and Easter, including the Advent and Lenten seasons that accompany them.

Friends observed certain principles of worship and ministry as a testimony to the truth. They regarded worship as essentially spiritual and not ceremonial. They drew this conclusion from Jesus' conversation with the Samaritan woman at Jacob's well about the nature of true worship; "God is spirit, and those who worship him must worship in spirit and truth (John 4:24). From this conviction arose the Quaker testimony against the outward observance of the sacraments of baptism and the Lord's Supper. Friends also had a testimony against the "hireling ministry" in favor of the "free gospel ministry." They believed they should be called of God to the ministry and inspired by the Holy Spirit for ministry, rather than be theologically trained from ministry. Meetings recognized and recorded gifts in the ministry, rather than ordaining persons in ministry as a class of persons set apart with special religious authority. Another witness of Friends was a testimony against creeds in the churches. Faith is a matter of first-hand religious experience and not a set of creedal beliefs to be repeated in unison during worship.

The most problematic and controversial of the early Quaker testimonies was Friends' opposition to music and the arts. Contrary to the practice of seventeenth-century Friends almost all Quakers today include music and the arts either in their worship, in their homes and family life, or in their schools. In the early history Friends were strongly influenced by the Puritan tradition which may partly account for their disavowal of music and the arts. But their chief reason was their firm determination not to let anything deter them from focusing attention on God's will for them. Friends did believe in the "inner music of the Spirit," but for them this was quite different from making music by humanly contrived means. Robert Barclay wrote: "The formal and customary way of singing has no foundation in scripture and no basis in true Christianity. And there is no precept or example for artificial music either by organs or other instruments in the New Testament" (Barclay, *Apology*, 298). If one was truly moved by the Spirit of God to sing in meeting for worship, that was accepted, but that did not include instrumental music because it was artificial.

When it came to the arts, Friends' objection was that art constituted a representation of reality rather than a first-hand experience of it. Why substitute a representation of that which one can experience directly and immediately? The principle involved here resembled that which caused Friends to renounce the sacrament of baptism and the Lord's supper. If one can have a first-hand experience of the baptism of the Holy Spirit, or if one can have direct communion with God in worship, then why depend on re-enactments and re-presentations of such events?

Some of the early Quaker testimonies may sound unfamiliar and forbidding to us now. In some cases we may practice them under other names. A typical list of Friends' testimonies today includes peace, simplicity, honesty, equality, community, and care for the environment. Undergirding all of these is the concern that our outward lives bear witness to truth discerned inwardly. It is in this framework of thought that the Testimony of Integrity needs to become the common denominator of all the other Quaker testimonies. The purpose of this study is to illuminate the Testimony of Integrity as the starting point for all of our outward concerns about life, especially, the Peace Testimony for which Friends are best known. If our inward leading is to be "doers of the truth," then integrity needs to be at the center of our being, at the center of our consciousness, and at the center of our outward witness.

George Fox, as the founder of the Quaker movement, is believed to have coined the phrase, "Let your lives speak." On Firbank Fell in northwest England today, where Fox preached to over a thousand Seekers a fortnight after his vision on Pendle Hill of "a great people to be gathered," the words, "Let your lives speak," are inscribed on a plaque mounted on a large rock called "Fox's pulpit." This rock overlooks a hillside meadow where the Westmoreland Seekers gathered to hear Fox's message. There is something sacramental about this admonition given by Fox. If a sacrament is an outward sign of an inward grace, or an outward sign of an inward spiritual commitment, then "letting our lives speak" is indeed an outward sacrament of an inward leading of the Spirit.

Another descriptive saying of Friends is that "Quakerism is a way of life," which is to suggest that the testimonies are the moral and ethical fruit of the inward leading of the Spirit. One of my students in a paper on the Quaker testimonies put it this way: "They arise more out of a concern for purity, holiness, consistency with divine order than from a passion for social justice." Because the testimonies have a religious base they might also be called the Quaker "articles of faith," but clearly for Friends it is faith that must be translated into action.

It has become commonplace for Friends today to talk about Quaker values, a term drawn from society at large to describe a kind of secularized version of religious faith commitments. Values are projected ideals or goals which are rationally determined, whereas Quaker testimonies are derived from religious faith and experience fashioned out of a life of prayer, devotion and worship, joined with spiritual discernment and commitment. It is the latter which seems more appropriate to Friends to espouse rather than an emphasis on values as a basis for Quaker faith and practice.

Earlier in this century Cecil Hinshaw performed an important service for Friends by describing early Quakerism as a movement of "Christian perfection" grounded in integrity. He wrote an important Pendle Hill Pamphlet on this subject, *Apology for Perfection*, No. 138. Quoting from another writing of Cecil Hinshaw:

The essence of early Quakerism is precisely in a demand for complete integrity of the individual in his relation to God, to other people, and to himself . . . Another way of expressing this thesis is the assertion that the beginning point of the religious pilgrimage of George Fox was the search for perfection . . . Early Quakerism was the first Protestant "holiness" or "perfectionistic" movement . . . George Fox cannot be understood apart from a recognition that the driving force in this life at this time was for complete integrity. With a passion that defies logic he demanded for himself and for others a life of holy obedience in even the smallest detail of life (Hinshaw, "Christian Perfection in Quakerism," 1-3).

Quakers as "Publishers of Truth"

The Testimony of Integrity is grounded in the early Quaker understanding of "Truth," often spelled with a capital "T." From the beginning Friends were known as "Publishers of Truth" and "Children of the Light," even before they were known as Friends or Quakers. Later Friends sometimes greeted one another by asking the question: "How is Truth prospering in thy parts?" which is to say, where you live. What a searching way to begin a conversation! It has the advantage of zeroing in on what is important. Friends were not given to idle talk.

The basic truth early Friends were talking about was not what ordinarily comes to mind. It is not propositional truth, or a philosophical view of correspondence or coherence, though it may well exhibit some of those characteristics. For Friends truth referred to the gospel life and the Spirit of the living Christ, which they found in the Christian Scriptures. George Fox described it this way:

> I was to direct people to the Spirit that gave forth the Scriptures, by which they might be led into all Truth, and so up to Christ and God, as they had been who gave them forth. And I was to turn them to the grace of God, and to the Truth in the heart, which came by Jesus . . . I was to bring people off from their own ways to Christ, the new and living way . . . to know the spirit of Truth in the inward parts, and to be led thereby . . . making melody in their hearts to the Lord (Fox, *Christian Faith and Practice*, 10).

In similar vein Thomas Ellwood said of Fox: "He was valiant for the truth, bold in asserting it, patient for suffering for it, unwearied in laboring in it, steady in his testimony to it, immovable as a rock" (Ellwood, *Christian Faith and Practice*, 12).

When Fox said he was to turn people "to the Truth in the heart," he intended to avoid at all costs a second-hand knowledge of God. He wanted to confront his hearers with the penetrating question, "What canst thou say?" Not what someone else says, or even what the Bible says. It must be the kind of truth that lays hold of us in a very personal way. It is truth which requires a response from us and will not let us rest until we have translated it into action.

Thus the truth Fox was talking about was truth to be obeyed. And because Fox believed that this truth "came by Jesus" as experienced by the early Quakers, it was truth to be obeyed according to the will of God as revealed in the life, teachings and ministry of Jesus. Integrity, therefore, involved discipleship and holy obedience. Jesus was seen as a personal embodiment of this kind of truth. Friends believed this was confirmed in the *Gospel of John*, when Jesus said: "I am the way, and the truth, and the life; no one comes to the Father [God], but by me" (John 14:6).

There is yet another way of describing this early Quaker view of truth, this time taken from the Hebrew Scriptures. The Hebrew word for truth, *emeth*, is sometimes translated "faithfulness" (e.g. Hosea 2:20; Deut. 32:4), meaning the trustworthiness, reliability and fidelity of Yahweh [God]. This was a characteristic of truth which was understood and proclaimed by early Friends. These observations about the biblical and early Quaker view of truth are important for our claim that the Quaker Testimony of Integrity is derived from the Quaker reading of the scriptural understanding of truth. The ground of religious certainty for

Friends was rooted in the gospel tradition and their belief in the faithfulness, dependability and trustworthiness of God. At the same time this view of truth was only authentic and real if it was grounded in a first-hand experience of the living God.

Plainness and Self-Denial

One of the most obvious manifestations of the Quaker view of truth was reflected in the early commitment of Friends to a lifestyle of "plainness and self-denial," and avoidance of the "vain and empty customs" of the world. Friends in the seventeenth century had been nurtured by the Puritan culture and ethic of their time. This probably accounts for much of their austere and strict way of life. But they were also convinced inwardly that their outward life must be liberated from the fashions of the day in order to follow the simple and unencumbered life of their Lord. They were committed to Jesus' saying: "If any man would come after me, let him deny himself and take up his cross and follow me" (Matthew 16:24).

William Penn in his famous *No Cross, No Crown* wrote that "the cares and pleasures of this life choke and destroy the seed of the kingdom, and quite hinder all progress in the hidden and divine life" (Penn, 204). Likewise, George Fox gave the same kind of advice to early Friends: "Keep all in modesty and plainness, fervency and sincerity and be circumspect. For they that follow those things, that the world's spirit invents daily cannot be solid. . . . Therefore, take heed of the world's fashions, lest you be moulded up into their spirit. That will bring you to slight Truth . . . (Fox, *Epistle* 250).

Early Friends were committed to "acting truth" in their daily lives. The source of their "acting" was not governed by outward laws and codes of ethics, but by the inward leading of the Spirit of Truth and the Light of Christ within. At the same time they were quite specific about what would keep them focused on the divine will and what would deflect their attention from it. They warned against drinking parties, sports and games, theatrical performances, and all sorts of frivolous entertainment. At the same time the Truth required that they be careful with their time, honest in their dealings, truthful in speech, faithful in the use of the plain language, " unadorned in dress and furnishing of their houses, and exemplary in their behavior. A double standard was to be avoided at all cost and nothing was "to divert the mind from the witness of God in the heart" (Barclay, *Apology*, 389). Thus they endeavored to live out the Quaker Testimony of Integrity as an essential part of their faith. Robert Barclay declared: "The chief purpose of all religion is to redeem men from the spirit and vain pursuits of this world, and to lead them into inward communion with God" (Barclay, *Apology*, 389).

The Quaker Practice of Integrity

The Testimony of Integrity can be articulated and practiced by Friends in four distinct ways.

• *The first is truth-telling, or simply not telling lies.* This is the most obvious place to begin to live out the Testimony of Integrity. Friends have always been known for truthfulness and honesty in their relationships and dealings with others. This standard of truthfulness was grounded in Jesus' and James' biblical injunction not to take an oath or to swear that one will tell the truth (Matthew 5:33-37; James 5:12). Friends were very conscientious about this, not only because taking oaths and swearing was forbidden by the Scriptures, but because it implied a double standard of truth, thus suggesting that when not under oath it is all right to lie. Friends' concern was that followers of Christ should be known for telling the truth all the time, and not just when one was called before a judge and sworn to tell the truth.

Webster's Dictionary defines an oath as "a ritual declaration, based on appeal to God . . . that one will speak the truth, keep a promise, remain faithful, etc." And swearing means to make a solemn declaration or affirmation (by invoking the presence of God as a witness) that now one will tell the truth. Contrary to this implied double standard, Friends believed in a single standard of truth and honesty. Even in merchandizing Quakers were known in England for the "one price system" because they did not believe in applying a double standard by having more than one price. Even children could be sent to a Quaker merchant and the parents could be assured that the child would not be cheated. On the other hand, many Quakers suffered persecution and imprisonment because they refused to exercise a double standard before judges in courts of law. Early Friends were thrown into jail more often for refusing to take the oath than for any other reason. Anybody who didn't like the Quakers could make a charge against them, have them arrested and brought before a judge, whereupon they were automatically thrown into jail, guilty or not, because they refused to swear that now they would tell the truth.

In Dietrich Bonhoeffer's book *The Cost of Discipleship*, there is a remarkable chapter on "Truthfulness" in which the author sounds more like an English-speaking Quaker than a German Lutheran pastor and theologian. Bonhoeffer was imprisoned during World War II for threatening the life of Hitler, and was hanged by the Nazis a few days before the end of the war. His chapter on "Truthfulness is a classic exegesis of Jesus' injunction not to insinuate a lie by swearing that one will now tell the truth under oath. Bonhoeffer held that "the very existence of oaths is proof that there are such things as lies. Oaths are intended as a barrier against untruthfulness." Further, he says that "perjury is a word for telling lies under oath." But Jesus destroys the lie by forbidding oaths altogether. There is no need for the oath if one speaks the truth in all circumstances (Bonhoeffer, 151-155). Jesus said, "Let what you say be simply 'Yes' or 'No'; anything more than this comes from evil" (Matthew 5:37). The Testimony of Integrity calls for truth-telling under all circumstances and at all times.

• *Second, Integrity calls for authenticity, for genuineness, and for veracity in one's personhood.* It calls us to be truly who we are and not be two-faced by trying to be something or somebody we are not. Some years ago our family saw a movie entitled, "Separate Tables." The one line I remember from it was the definition of a liar: "A liar is someone who tries to be something or somebody he/she is not." About the same time we had a neighbor who came home from a shopping spree one day with a new wardrobe of clothes. My wife asked her what was up; where was she going? She replied that she was going back to her *alma mater* for her twenty-fifth class reunion. Then she said, "You know, that is going to be one big lying session when we get back there!" So admittedly she was preparing, like all the rest, to put on her best front and try to be someone she wasn't. At least she was honest to admit the intent of her behavior.

The opposite of integrity of course is hypocrisy, which means phoniness, sham and deception. Jesus has some scathing words for hypocrites in Matthew 23. He declares seven woes against the religious authorities of his time, the Scribes and Pharisees, who were hypocrites and pretenders of virtue and piety. We are all tempted to become pretenders in this way. The tendency to misrepresent our true selves is a common shortcoming we all have, but we do not always realize that we are violating our integrity every time we respond this way.

• *Third, Integrity calls for obedience, or if you prefer, faithfulness to conscience illumined by the Light Within.* For Quakers this is the seat of religious authority and, therefore, the touchstone of our faith. Here Quaker truth and integrity take on an existential quality. It is truth which may well have objective validity, as I believe it does, but if it is not truth which is internalized in each of us, and for which we take ownership, then it is not truth which is valid and binding for us. But once it lays hold of us, it is truth that will not let us go until we have acted upon it. This kind of truth is new and fresh and therefore vital. It is not grounded in dogma, creeds, abstract philosophical ideas, or theological affirmations. It is not to be found in religious textbooks or Quaker books of discipline, but it is grounded in a living faith and experience of the present moment. It is the basis for the Quaker testimonies – the testimonies which are a living witness to the inward leading of the Spirit of God in our lives.

• *Fourth, the root meaning of the word "integrity" calls for wholeness.* The word comes from the Latin *integuitas*, which refers to a state or quality of being complete, that is, a condition of wholeness. The word "integrity" and the mathematical term "integer" all have a common meaning. When we look at this common meaning of *integritas*, or "integrity," it points to a unity, which when applied to persons, we call community. Integrity creates a sense of togetherness and belonging when applied to persons in community. Integrity forms the basis for a covenant relationship in which persons exercise a sense of responsibility and accountability toward one another. Individualism, which is preoccupied with doing one's own thing, often with little concern for how it affects other people, dominates much of our behavior in western society, and in our American culture in particular, and it affects the Religious Society of Friends as well. Thus, we need to recover the Testimony of Integrity, to balance this other attitude when applied to wholeness in the corporate life of persons where there is a sense of responsibility and accountability toward one another.

Examples of this kind of corporate integrity are of course reflected in Quaker testimonies, the origin and background of which we have already examined in some depth. Although these testimonies first arose out of the inward leadings of truth in the minds and hearts of individual Friends, the fact that Friends came to share similar leadings finally resulted in the common expressions and practices which we call testimonies. In the course of Quaker history Friends have experienced common leadings about many aspects of life which resulted in the united witness of their faith to the world.

Some of the best remembered corporate leadings of Friends from the past have included their concern for native American Indians when Quaker settlers, led by William Penn, came to Pennsylvania. Or we can recall Friends' deep concern for prison reform and for the improved treatment of the insane in both England and America.

Almost from the beginning Friends were conscientious about the education of their children in "all things civil and useful." Evidence of this corporate concern resulted in the development of many Friends schools at the elementary and secondary levels, and eventually at the college and post-graduate level.

From the end of the seventeenth century Friends worked for the civil and religious liberties of people through the establishment of Penn's "Holy Experiment" in government in Pennsylvania. This commitment to good government for the purpose of advancing human liberty has continued down to this day through the corporate witness of Friends, in the work of the Friends Committee on National Legislation in Washington, D.C., for example.

Quaker involvement in the world of business, commerce and industry has in the past often reflected the corporate philanthropic concerns of Friends. Historic examples include the Cadbury, Rountree and Fry family-owned factories in England where a cocoa product was processed as an alternative to drinking intoxicated beverages. But their concern went beyond the product to improving the living conditions of their employees. For example, the Cadburys in the Selly Oak district of Birmingham experimented with community housing and settlement projects to improve the economic and social needs of the workers.

Another example of the corporate witness and testimony of Friends has been their remarkable involvement in relief and rehabilitation work on behalf of victims of wars, natural disasters, economic deprivation, and social dislocation. Examples of this kind of relief work range all the way from the Spitalfields soup kitchens to feed unemployed silk weavers in East London in the seventeenth century, to the Irish potato famine relief in the nineteenth century, and to the massive relief and rehabilitation work of Friends' service agencies during and following the two world wars in this century.

From the beginning in the seventeenth century Friends' social customs of dress and address have reflected the way of simplicity and self-denial. Friends corporate witness to this way of life was spelled out in Robert Barclay's *Apology* (Proposition 15), and William Penn's *No Cross, No Crown*. Although the religious and social customs of Friends have changed over time, their corporate witness in such matters has made it possible for individual leadings to be tested by the members of the Meeting community.

There are also new concerns which arise to claim Friends' attention. Although Friends have always stood for the equality of men and women, there has been growing recognition among Friends of an imbalance between the treatment of the sexes, all too often favoring men over women. Thus, there is a resurgence of Friends affirmation of women's gifts and a growing concern to avoid sexist language. Likewise there is developing Quaker awareness of the lives of gays and lesbians so that they can be liberated from prejudice. These concerns and others constantly surface to claim Friends' attention in response to the inward spiritual leadings of truth. Only as Friends respond with a corporate sense of integrity to these emerging concerns can we expect to remain relevant to the needs of our time.

Integrity in its root meaning and search for wholeness leads to an even deeper sense of community than we have described so far. This level of wholeness goes beyond the community of persons to a spiritual community with "the ground of our being," to use the words of Paul Tillich. Here we need to associate integrity with the religious concept and experience of salvation. Now that may seem strange, because the word "salvation" is not fashionable anymore, except among radio and television evangelists, and a few Fundamentalist church folk. But according to Paul Tillich the root meaning of "salvation" can be derived from the Latin *salvus* (or *salus*), which means "health" or "wholeness." Surely all of us hope for health and wholeness in our lives, both physical and spiritual. If the wholeness aspect of integrity leads to a sense of community of persons, likewise it can lead us to an experience of spiritual wholeness in our relationship with God. This comes very close to what Saint Augustine meant when he prayed: "Thou hast created us for Thyself [Oh God], and our hearts are restless until they find their rest in Thee. " In a similar vein Olive Wyon writes, "integration is not an end to itself it is a means to an end, and the end is God" (Wyon, *On the Way*, 69).

The Lack of Integrity in Daily Life

We turn now to some of the specific ways in which the Testimony of Integrity is challenged in modern life. I believe that the world is hungry for integrity in daily life. As we look around us, we are overwhelmed by a culture which has few compunctions about lying, cheating and stealing. People's lives are fraught with hypocrisy, deception and fraud. Such behavior seems to be the norm. Let us enumerate some areas of life where standards of integrity are lacking or at risk.

The epidemic of drugs and drug dealing in the world today represents widespread disregard for integrity in personal conduct and human relationships. Here, for example, one is reminded of the indiscriminate use of steroids in order to increase one's energy and endurance in sports competition. Such addictions are certain to destroy long-term prospects for health, and they represent only the tip of the iceberg of the drug threat to our culture.

Another example of disregard for integrity is the insider trading and fraud practiced in the money centers of the world. Those who commit such deceptions seemingly have no sense of remorse or moral turpitude for their behavior, which sends shock waves through the market economy every time a new case is reported.

In the field of higher education colleges and universities find themselves in a highly competitive relationship to other institutions in intervarsity athletics, and in making application for research grants from government and private foundations. Although we may want to think well of such institutions, how can they become bulwarks for freedom and truth in our society when they, more often than they want to admit, become involved in unfair competition and misrepresentation of the truth in their intercollegiate and public dealings!

Turning to government and public policy-making, widespread use of lies, dirty tricks, and cover-ups in order to by-pass legal and democratic procedures in the interest of personal gain or acquisition of power and influence undercut integrity. All aspects of government, however, are not corrupt and evil, as some are inclined to believe. Quakers have long held that it is possible to work through government to help correct the wrongs of society and transform the world. But we are also aware of the way in which integrity is violated when the drive for personal power and the greed of special interest groups dominate the political scene.

Still other examples of lack of integrity confront us in the marketplace. We certainly know as consumers that every time we walk into a supermarket or a department store we feel unsure whether we are going to be cheated, either because of the questionable quality of the goods, or because we are unsure about the fairness of the price, or because the clerk's sales talk is exaggerated and not to be trusted. Sometimes we are not only victims of cheating and deception, but we find ourselves so enmeshed in the system that we inadvertently or unknowingly become allied with the untruthfulness that goes on. Whether or not we become perpetrators of this kind of wrongdoing, we are often tempted to lie and cheat (perhaps just a little!) because everyone else is doing it.

We also need to ask ourselves about our sense of integrity and fidelity in family relationships, in our dealings with our spouses and children. Some disturbing Quaker research suggests that violence in Friends' family life is not all that different from the violence which takes place in other similar groups in society. If this is the case, what kind of models are we for our children and for one another? Where is our moral conscience when such unseemly behavior touches us where it hurts the most, in our personal and family relationships?

Because of such widespread lack of simple honesty we are forced to ask the question: Is it not true that we are in about as much danger of being destroyed by our own moral sickness and culpability, as a society, as we are in danger of annihilation by a nuclear explosion! We are all concerned about the possibility of an accidental nuclear holocaust, as we should be, and we should not in any way detract from that concern. But is it not true that there is something else eating away at our society (and perhaps at humankind around the world) which should claim our attention and concern just as much as the nuclear threat?

The Clarion Call to Integrity and Veracity

Friends in the past set very high standard for themselves. In the beginning, as indicated earlier, they were committed to what Friends called "Christian perfection." This was a call to live up to the measure of the Light of Truth which is made available to us from day to day. It is a call to holy obedience to the Light of Christ within.

Friends need to remind ourselves of the words of the renowned Harvard psychologist and philosopher, William James, who describes Quakerism as "a religion of veracity, rooted in spiritual inwardness." He goes on to say that early Quakerism was "a return to something more like the original gospel truth . . . than had ever been known in England." This is a bold statement on our behalf. How well do we emulate it in our Quaker lives today (James, *Varieties of Religious Experience*, 8)?

The British Quaker, Hugh Doncaster, at the 1967 Friends World Conference at Guilford College, challenged Friends in his keynote address: "The world is dying for lack of Quakerism in action. " I agree, but I do not believe we are worthy of associating with such a claim unless we begin to take the Quaker Testimony of Integrity as seriously as we do the other Friends testimonies. We need to learn how to model our Testimony of Integrity in our personal, professional and vocational lives. We need to learn how to teach our children these testimonies. We need to begin to live the way we want the world to become, rather than the way the world is now. The crying need is for integrity in daily life, and Friends would do well to undergird all of their outward testimonies with the Testimony of Integrity, which must begin within the sanctuary of our own souls.

Reference Notes

Barclay, Robert. *Apology in Modern English*. Elberon, NJ: Privately published, 1967.

Bonhoeffer, Dietrich. *The Cost of Discipleship*. New York: The Macmillan Co., 1949.

Christian Faith and Practice in the experience of the Society of Friends. London: London Yearly Meeting of the Religious Society of Friends, 1960.

Hinshaw, Cecil. *Apology for Perfection* (Pendle Hill Pamphlet No. 138). Wallingford, PA: Pendle Hill, 1964.

____________________ "Christian Perfection in Quakerism." Unpublished lecture at Earlham School of Religion, Richmond, IN, 1974.

James, William. *Varieties of Religious Experience.* New York: The Modern Library, 1902.

Jones, T. Canby. *The Power of the Lord Is Over All*: The Pastoral Epistles of George Fox. Richmond, IN: Friends United Press, 1989.

Penn, William. *No Cross, No Crown: A Discourse Shewing the Nature and Discipline of the Holy Cross of Christ.* Philadelphia: T.K. & P.G. Collins, 1853.

Punshon, John. *Testament and Tradition: Some Aspects of Quaker Spirituality* (Swarthmore Lecture 1990). London: Quaker Home Service, 1990.

Wyon, Olive. *On The Way*. Philadelphia: The Westminster Press, 1958.

Pendle Hill Welcomes you

Pendle Hill is a residential study center as well as the publisher of Pendle Hill books and pamphlets. On an informal campus with paths, vegetable garden, and many fine trees, Pendle Hill offers a three term **residential program** from October to June for about 35 persons at any stage of life. About half the community are Quakers. Among the rest, a wide diversity of faiths, philosophies and backgrounds brings a richness to the dialogue of seeking.

Each morning community members gather in **meeting for worship**, held in the manner of Friends. Every community member participates in the **work program**, helping with upkeep of house and grounds and with food preparation and meal clean up. Pendle Hill offers six **courses** per term in areas including Quaker faith and practice, study of scripture, prayer, personal growth, peace and social concerns, literature and the arts. Spiritually focused craft and creative expression classes offer special opportunity for growth and healing.

Admission to this residential program is based upon the applicant's commitment to learning, and readiness to take a responsible part in the common life of Pendle Hill. **Financial aid** is available.

Pendle Hill also offers a full program of short-term events through its weekend and weeklong conferences and retreats; summer workshops; and a series of Monday evening lectures. Persons wishing a short-term experience in the resident community may come as **sojourners.**

Further details for all programs, dates, and fees are available from: *Information Services,* Pendle Hill, 338 Plush Mill Road, Wallingford, PA 19086-6099. Phone 1-800-742-3150.

Why Pamphlets?

If you are unfamiliar with Pendle Hill publications, why not start a subscription to the pamphlet series?

One of the basic ideas concerning Pendle Hill is the application of the tenets of the Religious Society of Friends to education as a preparation for usefulness in the field of religion and social action. Because it is a Quaker institution, Pendle Hill differs radically from a theological seminary or a school for social workers. As in the case of other vital movements, small or large, the idea motivating this experiment seeks embodiment in pamphlets. Pendle Hill pamphlets, like the early Christian or the early Quaker tracts, present a variety of viewpoints, all in some way derived from another fundamental idea. Variety is evidence of life; cold uniformity presages death.

But why pamphlets? Why not more books, or magazine articles, or posters? The typical pamphlet has certain characteristics which make it an apt vehicle for experimental thought. It should be the right length to be read easily at a single sitting (9,000 words). It should portray a single thesis without wandering from it. It must be concerned with a topic of contemporary (though not necessarily topical) importance. And a Quaker pamphlet, like a Quaker sermon, must embody a concern.

Though these qualifications have never been used as a systematic checklist by our Publications Committee in choosing manuscripts, they have generally applied to the more than 300 pamphlets we have issued since Vincent Nicholson's *Cooperation and Coercion as Methods of Social Change* began our series in 1934. Some of these pamphlets have been written by persons who have lived and worked at Pendle Hill as students and staff or who have attended conferences or visited as sojourners. Others come from a wider community of seekers.

Approximately 100 pamphlets are still in print. Those older pamphlets which have gone out of print are available in photocopied form. Please write to the bookstore for a catalog:

Pendle Hill Pamphlets Subscription Order Form

2002 Rates:
6 issues per year

	U.S., Canada, Mexico	Overseas Surface	Overseas Air
1 year	$16	$17	$23
2 years	$31	$32	$41
3 years	$45	$46	$58

Please enter my subscription:

Name ____________________

Street ____________________

City ____________________ State ________ Zip________

Country ____________________

❑ 1 year ❑ 2 years ❑ 3 years

Please enter my gift subscription:

Name ____________________

Street ____________________

City ____________________ State ________ Zip________

Country ____________________

❑ 1 year ❑ 2 years ❑ 3 years

Gift Card from ____________________

VISA and MasterCard accepted. Total $________

❑ Check enclosed ❑ VISA ❑ MasterCard

Name ____________________

Card Number ____________________ Exp. Date ________

Pendle Hill Bookstore
338 Plush Mill Road • Wallingford, PA 19086-6099
1-800-742-3150
bookstore@pendlehill.org or www.pendlehill.org